MARGO & GENEVIEVE

A love story

Written and illustrated by
Sallie Lundh

ISBN-13: 978-1717065285
 ISBN-10: 1717065287

For Matilda

*"I would venture to guess that Anon,
who wrote so many poems without
signing them, was often a woman."*
      — Virginia Woolf

Contents

Introduction

I am that kind of person who constantly builds up new worlds of daydreams to live in; I create cities, characters, friends, lovers — and I live with them until they no longer serve me any purpose. Then, I forget about them, and I let the story fade away and I build a new world.

This book is the story that never faded away. Margo and Genevieve came to me, as any other daydream, and they played out their sweet and wonderful (and, let's be honest, a little tragic) tale in my mind and when every scene, every chapter was played on the cinema screen behind my closed eyes, it was time to say goodbye —

Only, I couldn't. I could not let go. I had fallen in love with them, so I started writing it all down, resulting in this book that you are now holding in your hands.

The tale of Margo and Genevieve has lived inside of my head for half a year now, and it is time to let them go, but not in the way I usually let fantasies go. Their love story is to be read on caffées with your favorite hot drink by your side, curled up in a sofa wrapped in a soft blanket, on airports, or on a balcony in Paris.

I am letting them go — I am giving them to you.
Please take care of them.

Love,
Sallie

I
Pearly Girl

When perfection is a goal
it's hard to remain whole
for a human will be human
pretending to be a pearl;

Ready to love without heart
– to tear herself apart
trying to be a star, a moon, a sun!
though she is just a dressed up girl

The story has begun.

Margo

Margo doesn't have any flaws
  she is a photoshopped
magazine
  her life's a commercial
movie.

Oh, how perfect
a girl can be.

Perfect

Perfection
is a dream
a wish

a
life
goal

.

Daisy Game

She is a daisy
  in a white
  flower field.

Her friends
  are daisies
  surrounding
  her petals
    — bff's.

But what if the
  other daisies knew
  Margo's petals
  weren't actually
  white?

The Match

He is perfect they say.
  This is a perfect match.
  He is her friend's
  boyfriend's best friend.

You two will be
  the most perfect
  couple.

And our perfect Margo
  smiles and nods
  and takes his number.

Because if someone
  tells you "do this
  and you'll be
  p e r f e c t."

You listen to them.

Sports Radio

It is like talking
  to a sports radio.

Margo can only
  get her words out
  between the short pauses
  when he needs to inhale
  before a new cascade of
  sport and practise and
  technique
  drown her sentences.

"Isn't he just amazing?"
  her friends say.
"Oh, he is wonderful"
  she answers —
  *"I feel like we connect
  really well, and he is so
  easy to talk to."*

And her friends are excited
  because they found Margo
  her perfect match.

Absent Butterflies

There is something wrong with Margo. She can't feel the butterflies her friends talk about, can't feel the flutter in her heart. It seems like her friends are more in love with him than Margo is. *Is.* Because she *is* falling in love with him, right? They text. They talk. She laughs in the right places. Maybe the butterflies will come after they kiss. Yes. They will come after they kiss. They have to.

Out of Order

They never came,
  the butterflies.

He kissed her
  and all she felt
  was skin
   against skin.

Maybe I'm not
able to get those
feelings?
 Margo thought
 while smiling
 back at him.

Maybe my heart
 is already broken
 and I can't feel
 a thing.

Expected Answers

She was confused
 "This feels so right!"

She thought he was boring
(and a bit intimidating)
 "He is so fun to be with,
 he always makes me laugh!"

She wished that he would
 get tired of her.
 "I can't wait to see him again!"

      She wanted to
      escape this
      perfect
      life.

Autumn Leaves

He touched her
without asking
and she kept quiet
because this is
what boyfriends
and girlfriends
do together.

"How was it?"
her friends ask.

*His fingerprints
are burning inside
her body, they sting
when she move
her legs and
her intimate
flower petals
are about to
fall like dead
autumn leaves.*

"It was great!"

Goals

He wasn't a bad person. Because how could a bad person be so loved? All Margo's friends could talk about was how great her boyfriend was. Margo's parents adored him. The pictures on social media was, as they call it, *#goals*. After two months together they went out on a picnic. It was actually really nice. He talked about sports as always, but for a minute he was actually quiet, and Margo told him about her day. "That sounds nice," he said and put his arms around her, and Margo tried her best to enjoy his embrace. They listened to music (mostly from his playlist) and things felt, for once, good. *Until —*

— His hands were under her sweater, his breath in her mouth and her heart did flutter this time but not in the way her friends described it, but a flutter as if, if she was an animal, she would flee as far away as she could. But she wasn't an animal. She was a seventeen year old, confused, scared girl. The beach was empty, no one could see them, and even if someone did pass from far away, no one would understand that this was wrong. Because it wasn't wrong. Because in the eyes of everyone, they were a young couple in love. Because our perfect Margo wanted this to be passion so bad she was ready to fake it all, as long as the white, perfect walls of her life remained steady and tall.

Alcohol

Her body was a
free alcohol bar
and he surely
didn't let a single
drop of her
go to waste.

*His orgasm silenced
her screaming heart
and she couldn't wait
for him to go home
so she could take a
long*
    warm
        crying
            bath.

He never asked.
And she never said

"No."

Almost

Sometimes she could almost convince herself that she actually loved him. He was handsome, and funny and very, *very* charming. He bought her chocolate, and he always said "I love you" when they kissed goodbye. Her family wanted him over at their house all the time and her friends sighed enviously but satisfied whenever he hugged her in front of them. And in those moments, she almost felt that right flutter in her chest. Almost.

But the moments where she was alone with him and his friends, her chest crumbled like a paper bag. When the jokes that "are only jokes" drowned her and his hand slapping her behind while his buddies whistled and praised him for the "fine catch" put her in a cage of shame and embarrassment and the nights where she woke up with him inside of her — In those moments she hated him.

But he wasn't a bad person. He couldn't be.
They were a perfect match.

Distraction

"Girls night out!"

She wasn't just as excited
as her friends but she did
look forward to a party.

She brushed her long
sunshine hair and tried
not to think about that
he had tried to forbid
her from going.

*He was afraid that
Margo would meet
guys with the same mind
as his own.*

A phone call in a toilet booth

"Are you drunk?" He was angry.
"Not so you have to worry."
"I do worry, who are you with?"
"I told you, my friends."
"Are there any boys there?"
"At the party? Yes of course."
"I don't want you to be there."
"But I want to be here."
"Babe, you know I trust you,
  I just don't trust the boys
  and I don't like you being
  around a bunch of boys when
  I am not there."
"But I am not hanging out with
  the boys, I am with my *friends!*"
 "I need you to come home now."
 "Why?"
"Because if you don't,
  that means you are cheating on me,
  and then I promise I'll go and
  fuck the first hot girl I find.
  You know I can get anyone in bed,
  but I choose you."
"I am not cheating on you
  by being in the same room as boys!"
 "No, but they can do things to you,
  so if you choose to stay and somebody
  touches you, you have cheated on me."
"That doesn't make any s..."
"You get here now, Margo.
  My place, now."

And so she gave up. "Fine."
"Good, love you!"
 "Love you too..."

And they hung up.

Later, her friends would
"Awww!" when Margo
told them her boyfriend
missed her so terribly much
that she had to go home.

Genevieve

"So, do you?" she heard a voice say
from the booth beside her's.
"Do what?" Margo answered.
"Do you love him too?"

A head appeared over the edge
of the thin wall separating their
booths. Margo couldn't speak,
how rude can a person be?
The girl's face was covered in
black stripes *(she had been crying)*
but her smile sparked like fireworks.

"Hi there, I'm Genevieve."

The Perfect Place for Crying

"Hi, Genevieve, I'm Margo, and you are totally violating my personal space here." She looked up at the crying, smiling girl. "Are you standing on the toilet?"

"No, I'm just seven feet tall," Genevieve answered with a shrug. Margo stared at her. Genevieve rolled her eyes. "Yes, I am standing on the toilet." *Why did Margo's cheeks burn?* Why did she suddenly feel so embarrassed for asking a question, even if the question was pretty stupid? And why on earth did this small thing turn into this very big deal inside her head? She decided she did not like Genevieve, Genevieve made her uncomfortable. Then she decided to try making Genevieve feel uncomfortable too.

"Why are you crying in a toilet at a nightclub?" Margo asked.
"Am I?" Genevieve reached her hands to her black striped cheeks and laughed. "Oh, look at that. Right. I got my heart broken about twenty minutes ago and I figured a toilet in a nightclub was perfect for these dramatic feelings. You know, people are out there, having fun, while I sit here, alone, as my girlfriend — I mean ex, is out there with her tongue in somebody else's mouth. I don't know, I guess it felt like the perfect place for crying about life being unfair." Margo could not get a single noise out of her throat. Whatever the answer to her question could be, she did not expect *that*.

"Oh, I'm so sorry…"
"My ex is the one who should be sorry — I am amazing in bed, and very cute too." Genevieve's eyes got all watery again. "So why did she leave me for that *bimbo?*"

Right before Margo thought Genevieve was going to start crying again, Genevieve shook her head and fired off a wide smile.

"So, when is your lovely boyfriend coming to get you?" Margo woke up as from a dream. *She had to hurry.*

"He's not," she said while unlocking the door.

"What a gentleman." Margo heard how Genevieve jumped down from the toilet and suddenly she stood in front of her, blocking her way. "I need your number, text me so I know you got home safe."

Text

"I am safe" — *M.*

His body was heavy
  on her small chest,
  his arms suffocating
  every heartbeat.

Her phone: *pling*
  — a text.

Margo managed to
  reach a hand out of
  his duct tape grip
  and the message
  made her terrified
  and absolutely
  blissful.

"Sweet dreams, Margo
  tell me if you want to
  hang out someday" — *G.*

A little bumblebee
  was fluttering in
  perfect Margo's
  confused heart.

Hesitancy

A week past.
  Two weeks pasts.

Margo had lost count
  on how many times
  she had brought up
  her phone to text
  Genevieve
  but for some reason
  this small action
  felt a lot bigger than just
  saying hi to a new friend.

On Wednesday,
  the third week after
  the party, he decided
  to take Margo (and his friends)
  to the cinema and Margo
  decided to forget
  Genevieve

Popcorn

Margo couldn't remember the name of the movie, but it was something he chose (so it would fit his friends interests). They were meeting at the cinema, and when Margo came there she heard loud noises, mostly his voice. He was angry about something, the person he was yelling at (who also yelled back at him) had apparently (accidentally) pushed down his popcorn to the ground.

"Do you *see* how many people there is here? You can't just put your popcorn at the very corner of a small table if you don't want anyone to bump into it" a girl's voice said, loud but calm.

"Bitch you have to, you will buy me a new box of popcorn!" *That's his voice.* Margo tried to get passed the other guests as fast as she could, but the girl was right, the place was crowded.

"Maybe I would have considered buying you a new box of popcorn if you hadn't yelled *fucking bitch you're dead* as soon as your precious popcorns fell out across the floor, but now? No way." Where had Margo heard that voice?

"Fucking lesbo." The girl laughed, and Margo finally knew. *Genevieve.*

"Is that an insult or is your gay-radar just really good?" Margo just *knew* Genevieve was rolling her eyes in a very provocative way. *Oh my, oh no, she is pissing him off.*

"Do us all a favour and get some dick, maybe some real sex can make you shut up, you ugly unsatisfied slut."

"Unsatisfied? Sweet boy, if you don't how how lesbians have sex, I feel very sorry for whoever your girlfriend is."

Right after that sentence Margo managed to come through the wall of people that had been blocking her way and the disappointment in Genevieve's eyes and the shame in Margo's heart when he put his arm around her shoulders would sting like a wasp bite in her chest for the whole evening, and she got angry with herself, because she couldn't understand why.

Lies

"Really?" — G.

Margo wanted to explain herself,
  say that she was sorry.
  Margo wanted to tell Genevieve
  about a perfect life that isn't
  that perfect after all.
  Margo wanted to ask how Genevieve
  could make Margo's emotions curl like
  small tornadoes.
  Margo wanted to yell at Genevieve
  because she was confusing her.
  Margo wanted to replace the heavy arm
  around her shoulders with Genevieve's
  knitted red sweater.

How is it possible to want someone
  you never even touched?

Margo wanted to keep
  her perfect life.

"I love him. He is kind." — M.

If Margo's phone was a lie detector
  it would blink red and shout like a fire alarm.

Love Him

I do love him.

She dreamed about
 soft kisses and
 honey thighs.

I do love him!

She dreamed about
 warm embraces and
 starry eyes.

I do... Love him?

She dreamed about
 true love and
 sweet lips.

I don't love him.

Midnight Confession

Margo confessed something
  to herself that night, and
  her heart had never felt
  more heavy.

I never loved him.

?

How do you leave
  the perfect life
  ?

How do you end something
  when everyone around you
  is watching
  and judging
  your every
  step
  ?

How do you know
  if the imperfect
  is worth
  fighting
  for
  ?

Trying

The following month
  she tried.

She tried telling him
  no.

She tried sending Genevieve
  a text.

...

He never heard her
  no.

And Genevieve never got
  her text.

But she tried.
  Oh how she tried.

Anger

There is an emotion
  breaking through
  a person's chest
  when the *fear*
  is pretending to be *brave*
  and one day Margo's fear
  put up a whole act —

Her parents wanted Margo
  to walk in her father's footsteps
  but it's her life!
  Her friends wanted Margo
  to be slender as a mannequin
  but it's her choice!
  Her boyfriend wanted Margo
  to move like a puppet under his words
  but it's her body!

The emotion is called
  a n g e r
  — perfect Margo doesn't
  get angry, but it was enough
  for her to do a small, huge thing:

"Do you still want to hang out?" — M.
"I never thought you would ask" — G.

Escaping

"Paris? Now?" Genevieve looked at Margo as if Margo had told her the sky is chequered. Margo was actually quite satisfied over the fact that she had made Genevieve speechless.

"I need to escape. Just escape everything."

"Okay... I can understand that. But *Paris?* Have you thought of like, I don't know, *money?*"

"Genevieve, this very sweater that I am wearing was $600, money is not my problem."

"So you are asking me, someone who actually has a job and need those money to, you know, *survive,* to help you, a spoiled rich man's daughter, to use her I-had-the-luck-to-be-born-in-a-rich-family-privilege against her parents will and go to Paris?"

Margo felt her heart getting heavy.

"...yes?"

Genevieve stared at her for two infinities. Then she laughed, she laughed as if her lungs were filled with pop rocks.

"Hell yeah, I'll go to Paris with you."

2

Infatuation

One heart that were
for too long unheard
let out her every word;

Love sneaked in
under their skin
gingerly; so tenderly
wondering
— where have you been?

So she found
a heart that could
listen and who
understood.

Falling in Love

It is called *falling* in love because you have absolutely no control when it is happening, it's like tripping over a rock and you either fall down and land smoothly in the most beautiful meadow or you crash your whole soul on some hard concrete floors, and you never know what it is going to be until you're already there. Our perfect Margo thought she lacked the ability to fall in love, so when she fell, she tried to grab everything that was available, she did all in her power to keep her balance, but the clouds slipped through her fingers and the walls were too flat to hold on to — *Is it possible to walk away in the middle of a fall?*

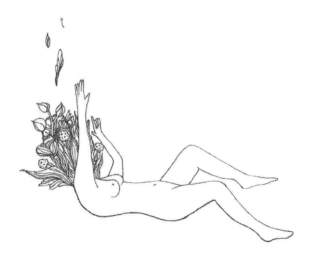

30 000 *ft*

Day one
The airplane's engines
  started moving and a hand
  grabbed onto Margo's arm.

"Have you never travelled
  by plane?" Margo asked.

Pure fear and a little bitterness
  sparked in Genevieve's eyes.

"I have, when I was like three
  and stupid and didn't know I
  was 30 000 ft over the ground."

Not Cool

"Genevieve, are you scared?"

"Of dying? *Yes.*"

"But we won't die."

"You don't know that."

"Yes, I do."

"Okay then, promise me one thing."

"What?"

"If we are about to die, you'll kiss me before we hit the ground."

"Okay."

"Really?"

"Yes, because we won't die."

"Kind of want to die now."

"Shut up, Genevieve."

"Make me shut up, Margo."

"That doesn't work."

"Too bad."

"Do you know that the seat belts aren't actually there to save you, but to make it easier to identify your body after a crash."

"Not cool, Margo, NOT COOL."

The Brave One

The sunrise over a sleepy Paris
  was quite something.
  Margo tried to make Genevieve
  look out the window —

"Nice try, I am not opening my eyes
  until I can feel the ground under us."

And so Margo enjoyed the view
  and the feeling of her being the
  brave one, even if it's only above
  the clouds.

Rose Gold

Day two
One hotel room and two beds
  with puffy pillows and rose gold sheets
  big window doors leading out to a balcony
  with colorful flowers and Eiffel Tower view
  and a bathroom with two beautiful bathtubs

  — and Margo would share all this with
  Genevieve *(she couldn't believe it)*
  Margo and Genevieve would share Paris
  with each other until day ten.

A Date

"Are you hungry?"
"Are you asking me out?"
"Genevieve, we have to eat."
"You're taking me on a date?"
"No, we need *breakfast.*"
"Yes, I will gladly go on a date with you."
"Are you going to be like this the whole time?"
"You like it, Margo."
"Shut up, Genevieve."
"Make me shut up, Margo."
"Not *again.* Come on now, let's go find a café."
"Oh my god, a café date in Paris,
 this is so romantic!"
"You are unbelievable."
"I know, you love it."

Margo shook her head as a no,
 but her smile said something else.

Split

They went on three dates that day
  according to Genevieve, and Margo
  gave up on trying to protest —
  after all, she didn't mind calling
  this trip a long, beautiful date.

But there was a sting in Margo's chest
  as if she was torn in two different directions,
  one led to her perfect life, her parents, her friends,
  even *him,* because that was all she knew —
  and the other one led to Genevieve.

Did she actually have the courage
  to go through with this?
   — Did she dare trying
  to walk the path
  she chose for herself?

Damn it, Margo

At the hotel.
Genevieve wanted to
  call her dad, so she sat
  on Margo's bed as the
  phone was stuck on
  the wall on that side.

Margo decided to
  take a shower and
  when she got out
  Genevieve was
  asleep on Margo's
  bed.

She probably fell asleep there on purpose!
  Go on, you can lay next to her,
  after all it is your bed!
  Damn it, Margo.

Margo put a blanket
  over Genevieve
  and went to sleep
  in the other bed.

Musée d'Orsay

Day three
"You're so gay..."
"What?"
"Hey, don't interrupt me!"
  Genevieve took a deep breath —
 "You're so gay, let's go visit
    musée d'Orsay!"
"I have a boyfriend."
 Why did she say that?

Was it Margo's imagination
  or did a flash of pain reach
    Genevieve's eyes?

"Don't you dare spoil my poetry!"
 "Genevieve, that was bad rhyming."
 "No, it was a poem, now,
    who is your favorite,
    Monet or Van Gogh?"
"I don't know."
Genevieve actually looked kind of sad now.
 So Margo continued —
"Let's take a route to musée d'Orsay
    and find out!

Genevieve's smile was back.
 "And you call *my* rhyming bad?"

Art

Genevieve was art.

They spent five hours
  on musée d'Orsay
  but the only masterpiece
  Margo was drawn to
  was the girl with the
  sunshine smile and
  chocolate cosmos eyes.

Touch the Artwork

Genevieve noticed
 (of course) Margo's
 gazing eyes —

"Oh yes, my level of pretty
 gets high as a rock star
 smoking cannabis when I am
 surrounded by famous paintings,
 you know the signs
 please do not touch the artwork
 doesn't apply to me so you are
 more than welcome to do more
 than just look at me like..."
"Shut up, Genevieve."
"Make me shut up, Margo."

Margo was annoyingly aware
 of how close Genevieve's face was,
 and she *almost* made her shut up,
 she *almost* leaned forward
 — their lips *almost* touched

but Margo turned around
 *— she had never been so
 disappointed in herself.*

The Eiffel Tower

Day four
The Eiffel Tower

Genevieve's facial expression
  while looking out over the view
  of Paris from the highest top of
  the Eiffel Tower was the most
  powerful sight Margo had ever seen.

Genevieve was actually *jumping*
  up and down from all the feelings,
  one could see how all her emotions
  bounced like basketballs inside of
  her body.

Margo couldn't stop smiling.

Peck *(n) a brief kiss*

It all went by so quickly
  Margo's heart didn't even
  react fast enough to skip a

b   a t
   e   .

"Margo!"
  and so Genevieve
  kissed her.

It wasn't a romantic kiss,
  it didn't last longer than a
  half second, but the seconds
  after were dizzy and cloudy.

"Thank you! Thank you
  so much, Margo!"

Genevieve turned against
  the pretty view again and
  Margo leaned against the wall
  — she had never been so drunk
  that her balance failed her
  but she could imagine this is
  what they mean when they say
  "The room is spinning."

Maybe

Margo had been kissed
 by girls before — by her friends,
 but those "Bff"-selfie kisses
 were nothing *(n o t h i n g !)*
 compared to Genevieve's.

How can the exact same kind
 of kiss feel so different?

How can a kiss that wasn't even
 a real kiss grow a blooming
 garden in her stomach?

Maybe I am able to
 get butterflies
 after all.

Bread, Coffee and Sweets

Day five

A small café with blood red neon letters shining *"Ouvert/ Open"* over the entrance — a door in dark wood with carved in nature pattern and window boxes filled with pink and white flowers.

When you walk in you feel like you stepped into an enchanted forest, with the fir-tree green walls decorated with paintings of mighty waterfalls, colorful birds and snowy mountains and hundreds of tiny lamps lighting up the room like fireflies amongst all the plants. The air smells like bread, coffee and sweets.

In the corner of this café, you can spot two girls, different like day and night — the fiery one, *the sun,* ordered a big milkshake mixed with white chocolate, oranges and whipped cream together with a golden croissant filled with apricot jam and nutella. The humble one, *the moon,* ordered a cappuccino with a little cocoa on the top together with a strawberry pie.

A date. *The tenth, actually.*

Intentions

"Margo?"

"Hm?"

"What are you trying to do?"

"What do you mean?"

"You know what I mean. What are
you trying to get out of all this?"

"I told you. I needed to get away
from everything."

"But why with *me?* Why not with
one of your friends?"

"They wouldn't understand."

"But they're your best friends?"

"It's complicated, Genevieve."

"No it's not, just tell me what you want."

"What do you want me to answer?"

"I want you to talk to me about what *this is.* "

"Genevieve..."

"You *like* me, Margo, *do* something."

"I don't understand what you..."

"You understand perfectly, Margo."

"But..."

"Tell me you don't like me."

"What?"

"Tell me you don't want me, Margo."

"I can't... I can't do that."

"So what are you so afraid of?"

"...everything."

Sugar Daddy

"Are you *sure?*"
"Genevieve, *stop asking that.*"
"But these shoes are *Chanel.*"
"When I told you that we are going
  shopping and that I'll pay for it all
  you promised not to look at the prices,
  stop looking at the prices."
"This is so irresponsible."
"Is that a problem?"

Genevieve took the shoe box
  and held it against her chest.

"Margo, my very own sugar daddy,
  this may go against my whole view
  of money, but what's bad for the wallet
  is apparently good for the soul!"

"Truer words have never been spoken,
  now, let's go find some dresses —
  we can't party in Paris without wearing
  highest level of fashion."

~~Love~~

Day six
Doing nothing
  together with
  the person you
  ~~love~~ like is a
  very satisfying
  occupation.

They spent the day
  with face masks,
  baths and doing
  each other's hair.

When the evening came
  they looked like goddesses
  prepared to hit the club.

Song of the Roses

Neon lights—

Blue: Margo's glittery dress with moonshine sequins sparkling like dancing stars through the music, a cyan colored drink in her hand and indigo eyeshadow; A magic peafowl disguised as a girl.

Purple: Genevieve's velvet jumpsuit, sunset laugh and mulberry earrings, moving hips and shining skin — she had covered herself in a body lotion that made her sparkle as if she was a violet diamond; A fiery fairy.

Pink: Two bodies drawn towards each other like magnets, soft innocent touches so powerful the loud music faded away, and in an ocean of a hundred partying people these two girls were the only ones who existed.

Red: Burning hearts longing to merge into one single throbbing emotion, calling out to one another and singing the silent but strong song of the roses while unkissed souls are waiting for their moment; *Love.*

Roof of Stars

Two stormy hearts
  walk hand in hand
  with alcohol bubbles
  in their blood and
  lovebirds in their chests.

A man is playing music
  in a corner of the street
  and Genevieve's hand
  is now on Margo's waist
  and they dance under
  a roof of stars.

"*Of course* you're taking the
  man's role when we slow dance."
"No, Margo, I'm no man."
"But you lead?"
"That's because I am a leader."
"How do you do that?"
"What?"
"How do you believe
  in yourself so much?"
"Let's just say that once I didn't
  and then I proved myself wrong."

And so Margo did

"Margo, you're not dancing to the music."
"What are you talking about? I dance perfectly fine."
"No, you dance like an old lady with a wooden leg."
"I do not!"
"It's cute, though."
"Shut up, Genevieve."
"Make me shut up, Mar..."

And so Margo did.

Three Waves

Margo's lips met Genevieve's
like when the ocean hits
the seashore after a storm —

The first wave throws itself at the waterfront so fast and powerful Margo even surprises herself, as if her heart suddenly decided to take over her whole being without asking what's right or wrong. When she pulls back, a few grains of sand *(Genevieve)* follow Margo's raspberry spirit breath, dragging her back to the shore; *The second* wave isn't hitting the bank as hard as the first, but it's filled with a strong current of burning desperation — a too thin fishbowl had been keeping too much water inside it's round fragile walls, so when it finally bursted from the heavy weight of longing, a waterfall cascaded through Margo's heart, and she could feel a volcano explode inside Genevieve's; *The third* wave is a satisfying aftertaste. It caresses the coast with smiling kisses and Margo never wanted it to end — nothing in the known universe had ever been so unreal and real at the same time.

Never

"I'm sorry..."
"For what?"

Margo tried to answer
 but the lump in her chest
 got stuck in her throat
 and all she could say was

"You know..."

Genevieve was quiet
 for a while, and Margo
 prepared herself to be
 yelled at, but to her
 great surprise the girl
 who's arms she was
 embraced in, put her
 face between her hands
 and kissed her softly.

"Margo, *never*
 apologise for not
 wanting to have sex.
 Do you hear me?
 Not to anyone. *Never.*"

Crime of Sweet Dreams

After a few kisses
  and a few cuddles
  Margo fell asleep
  in Genevieve's arms.

She did not know
  (oh what a crime
  of sweet dreams)
  that Genevieve was
  unable to turn away
  unable to stop watching
  unable to stop smiling
  unable to stop feeling—

Margo did not know
  that Genevieve stayed
  awake for hours and hours,
  too happy to fall asleep.

Rosewood

Day seven
When Margo woke up that morning
  her heart felt sparkly and light —
  when she danced with Genevieve
  it had melted like sugar and while
  she slept it had crystallized into
  a throbbing diamond.

Without waking up the sleeping girl
  beside her, Margo got out of bed and
  went into the shower —

Margo wrapped her hair in a towel
  put on a rosewood bodysuit and went
  back with a tourist map in her hand
  to a newly awake Genevieve.

"Genevieve, what do say about
  a picnic in Jardin du Luxembourg?"

Genevieve's jaw dropped and she was
  quiet for so long Margo started to feel
  uncomfortable. "My goodness,
  Genevieve, say something."

And so Genevieve grabbed Margo's
  waist, dragged her back into bed
  and kissed her with such intensity
  Margo's head turned into a pink cloud
  and her cheeks turned into cherries.

"...well said."

Jardin du Luxembourg

"Genevieve, what is your favorite place?"

The sun caressed their intertwined fingers and the air around them made candy floss grow in both of their minds.

"Right here, with you."

Margo's heart twinkled like sunshine on a wavy sea.

"No, I mean, well, *before this?*"

"Before you? I guess, the café where I work, the owner is my dad's best friend and we are like a little family."

"That sounds so nice."

"What is yours?"

"I don't know..."

The bathtub where I can lock myself in and wash him off.

"My room, I guess."

Photographs

They showed each other old photographs
  of themselves from when they were children.

Margo's favorite one is where Genevieve
  is five years old, and she sits on her father's
  shoulders — even as a child Genevieve's smile
  out shined the very sun — and they both had
  purple, glittery nails.

"Oh yeah, my dad always painted my nails,
  and I painted his so that we could be pretty
  together, so it would be fair."

"Couldn't your mum do it?"

"My mum left, she was never the family type,
  she tried, for me, but after I turned two she left
  and I haven't heard from her. I hope she's happy."

"Oh, I'm so sorry..."

"Don't be, Margo, I'm not. I have my dad,
  and he is great. You'll see when you meet him."

Coffee-tea

Sadness crawled up Margo's spine when Genevieve told her about her dad, because memories with Margo's own father started to fill her head —

A four year old Margo tries to give daddy a cup of tea. Of course it's not real tea, it is a small, empty porcelain cup.
"Daddy, I made tea!"
"Not now, sweetie."
"But daddy, it's daddy's favorite tea!"
"Daddy drinks only coffee, you know that."
"But it is *coffee-tea!*"
"Not *now*, Margo." he patted her small head before his face turned away, away from Margo, away from her tea, towards the tv.

A nine year old Margo asks daddy if he can braid her hair before her friends birthday party.
"Ask your mum."
"But mummy is sleeping."
"Then let it be as it is."
"But it is everywhere."
"It's pretty, Margo. Let it be."
"Can I cut it off?"
"Your beautiful hair? Never, don't you want to be pretty?"
"Yes but... I want braids..."
"It's prettier this way, Margo."
"Okay."

A twelve year old Margo just had her first period and is now standing in a grocery store, lost and confused.
"Dad..."

"Yes, Margo?"

"Can you help me? I don't know what to..."

"Margo, if you are talking about your lady problem, shut it, didn't your mum tell you what it is that you need?"

"Yes but, I forgot which ones, there are so many pads and..."

"*I don't want to hear about that.* I'm a man, it's disgusting, ask the staff."

With red cheeks and shame in her stomach, Margo took the first pack of pads she saw and made sure her father barely had to see the package.

Childhood

There was a difference between
  Margo's childhood photographs
  and Genevieve's —

Genevieve's childhood was:

1. Sometimes blurry

2. Messy in the background

3. Filled with smiles that wrinkled
    her face so much she almost looked
    more ugly than cute.

4. Pure and true.

Margo's childhood was:

1. Set up

2. Upright

3. Formal

4. Perfect

A Couple

Despite the stinging memories,
 the seventh day turned out to be
 one of the best days Margo had
 ever had in her whole life.

The warm flowery wind danced
 in their hair, while kisses were
 shared between giggles and smiles —

They were not Margo and Genevieve
 They were not the broken and the whole
 They were not the cautious and the brave
 They were not the rain and the sun
 They were not anxiety and bliss

They were
 a couple.

Notre Dame

Day eight

This day Margo and Genevieve took a walk in the rainbow light shining through the mighty windows inside Notre Dame. Margo had her hands in her pockets, she was unsure if the other people strolling around under the high decorated ceiling would react... okay, to two girls holding hands. After all, they were in a church. Margo had never really thought about God, she never believed in him, and that's that. But now, surrounded by people who clearly do believe in him, she could not withstand not asking Genevieve, if *she* believed in this divine being, and if so, did he hate them?

"Well, I myself am, as you may have figured, a lesbian goddess, so I have never really felt close to any *god...*"

"Genevieve, I'm serious, I want to know what your thoughts are."

"My thoughts? You want me to be deep? Alright, let's put it this way; I do not believe in the kind of God that is introduced in the Bible, I mean it was literally written by some old men in a time where the women basically were the men's property. *But* I have chosen to believe, or at least *try* to believe, in the God my dad believes in."

"And what kind of god is that?"

"Basically the same God, but this one is not strict and he doesn't think love of any kind is a sin. As long as you are happy and don't hurt anyone, my dad's God is welcoming you into his heaven after you die. Oh, that's another, or well, to be honest, *the biggest* and probably the most selfish, reason for why I really hope my dad's God exists; I don't want it to turn into a black nothing when I die, I don't want to believe that last year's christmas was the very last time I saw my grandma, I want to see her again. I want to believe that the people you lose aren't lost forever, you know? It's quite hard though, to believe in something that you have never seen, but I am trying, because I want it to be true. Because if there's anything I am afraid of, it is death. I really, *really* don't want to die. My dad believes that God creates people just as he wants them to be, which means we don't have to be *fixed,* everyone is already fine just the way they are, and I have no trouble with being completely in love with that thought, I wouldn't mind at all if my dad was right. It's sad though, that religion so easily is used in such violent ways, I mean, threatening people who doesn't follow your beliefs and saying that they are doomed to endless torture in hell? That is just fucked up."

"That... sounds quite nice actually. The part where everyone can do what makes them happy as long as they don't hurt anyone, I mean. Simply being a decent human being should be enough reason not to go to hell. What does your dad's heaven look like?"

"He thinks heaven is different for different people. It depends on what makes you happy. He is aaaaall about love and happiness, my old man. It's almost a little irritating sometimes. But mostly sweet."

Margo took one of her hands out of her pockets and reached for Genevieve's.

Not Enough

The closer they
  came to the tenth day, the bluer
  Margo's heart became.

I am not brave enough.
  I am not good enough.
  How can I be strong
  when I am way too weak
  for what is to come?

She had to make a choice.
  Soon.

Morning Cuddles

Day nine

24 hours left —

Genevieve was still asleep when Margo turned around, rested her head on the pillow while watching Genevieve's face.

Genevieve was the strong one, she was everything Margo wanted to have and what Margo wanted to be, but in her sleep Genevieve, for once, looked vulnerable; one could see that she wasn't an angel after all — but human. A very angelic human.

Margo reached her hand out, slowly following Genevieve's features with her finger, over the smooth eyebrows, across the nose, the lips and —

Suddenly Genevieve's hands were in Margo's hair and Margo moved closer and they kissed, and Genevieve was an angel again and Margo's heart dropped because she wanted this to last forever, she wanted to live in between these very sheets together with Genevieve, she wanted this moment to be their home for eternity and she wanted to kiss Genevieve even more after every kiss they shared.

Purple & Pink

16 hours left —

Two bathtubs
Two bodies
Two hearts

Hot water is embracing them
  while bath bombs tickle their skin
  (Genevieve's: purple. Margo's: pink)
  and hands reaching over the tub edge
  with fingers playing tag.

"Margo, are you looking at my boobs?"
"What?" for half a second Margo's eyes
  slipped down from Genevieve's face. "No!"
"You just did!" Genevieve's voice was filled
  with thrilled, proud, victory.
"That's not fair, you tricked me!"
"Whatever you say, Margo, whatever you say."
"Oh, shut up Genevieve."
"Make me shut up Margo."

That's it.
Margo crawled out of her bathtub
  and moved over to Genevieve's
  letting the purple water drown
  the small pink raindrops on her skin
  while pulling a slightly shocked Genevieve
  closer so that they were skin to skin, intertwined
  sitting between each other's legs.

Genevieve's eyes were big as two moons —
"Margo, you don't *have* to,
you said you didn't want to..."
"Oh, *I want to,* now let me make you shut up,
 Genevieve."

When the honesty in Margo's voice
 reached Genevieve's ears,
 a smile spread across her face,
 as she answered;

"Gladly."

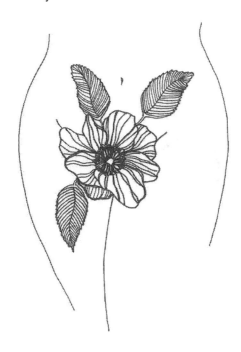

After

The lilac water turned cool
  while two hearts calmed down
  and a thousand goosebumps
  lowered their hills like treasures
  back down into blushing skin.

It became cold
  but neither of them
  were freezing.

Marigold Clouds

10 hours left —

They sat on the balcony watching the sun slowly fall asleep behind marigold clouds, and Margo could feel her heart sink down together with the daylight, how it hide under the asphalt trying to forget the reality that crawled against them *— this is our last night.*

Margo could feel the anxiety move around inside of her, like a fat snake with rough skin inside her stomach.

Porcelain

9 hours left —

"Why are you so quiet?"
"I'm tired."
"Nothing's wrong?"

Margo's ribs shattered
  one after one like porcelain
  leaving her chest unprotected
  — and her heart grew a layer
  of stinging frost.

"No." She kissed Genevieve,
"No, everything's fine."

I am a coward
  and you will hate me.

Please

6 hours left —

Margo watched how
  Genevieve's chest slowly
  calmly; *peacefully*
  moved up — down.

𝒰*p*

     —

       down.

"I am so sorry"
  one heart whispered
  to another; "Please,
  please, understand."

Wifi Blues

5 hours left —

She connected her phone
  to the hotel's wifi and
  messages from her friends
  her parents — from *him*
  blew up the screen,
  every vibration more painful
  than the one before; *reality*.

She only sent a text to one person:

"I hope you found the note,
  please, can you pick me up
  at the airport tomorrow?

I'll explain everything
  in the car.

Love, Margo."

Selfish

Day ten
2 hours left —

Genevieve woke her up with a breakfast tray filled with golden bread, port salut cheese, grapes, raspberries and juice; "I thought we could eat breakfast in bed today, so I went down to the hotel's kitchen and asked for it and look how pretty they laid it out!" Margo smiled and kissed Genevieve when she crawled up beside her back in bed placing the food between them — for a moment everything was fine, she was in Paris, eating breakfast together with her girlfriend, and they were in love, and happy and —"...I thought it would be nicer like this, only the two of us, since it's our last day in Paris, you know." *Our last day.*

Margo nearly coughed up her heart, no — she *did* cough up her heart, *and the heartstrings got stuck in between her teeth together with the pulp from the juice and —*

"Margo, are you really okay?"

Tell her! Margo's brain shouted. *Tell her!* Margo's heart begged.

"Actually, Genevieve, there's something..." but the words couldn't make it past her teeth, couldn't escape the sticky remains of her heart, and she hated herself for it, she hated herself for doing the most selfish thing anyone could ever do; she would enjoy every last minute together with Genevieve, until she broke both of their hearts.

"... you're just so beautiful."

Genevieve fired off that firework smile of hers;

"Well, I knew *that,* silly. Now, taste one of these grapes, they are almost as sweet as you are!"

Stand Still

One hour left —

Paris airport
  a crowded gate
  and a bag filled
  with silent agony.

43 minutes left —

Genevieve is taking
  a nap with her head
  resting on Margo's lap.

Oh, dear time,
  please stand still.

28 minutes left —

An airplane window
  framing the sky over
  the city where Margo
  found true love.

A girl by her side — *Genevieve*
  holding her heart
  unaware of what
  is to come.

Masquerade

10 minutes left —

Sometimes it is the most simple things
  that are the most complicated; *Love*
  — to stay, to leave,
  to continue this masquerade
  or to bow, wave; get off the stage.

Time never waits for decisions,
  no matter how big they are.

5 minutes left —

"Genevieve?"
"Yes, Margo?"
"Promise me
  something?"
"Anything."

"Kiss me,
   before
        we
           hit
              the
                  ground."

Water Glass

10 seconds left —

Ten... Nine... The airplane is moving faster and faster and faster, Genevieve is once again grabbing on to Margo's arm, and Margo is grabbing on to Genevieve's, because this time, *Margo is afraid too.*

Eight... Seven... Six... They hold on to each other, one simply afraid of flying, and one afraid of the destiny of their destination; Fear is making Margo see and feel everything in slow motion and fast forward all at once, it is like watching a water glass fall — you *know* there's no other option than wait for it to crash down and spread its shards across the floor before it's even possible to clean up the mess.

Five... Four... Margo's heart is the water glass. The airplane swings, thundering over its last seconds in France, soon leaving the ground — *can a fall begin with a journey that goes up?*

Three... "Margo?"
"Yes?"

Two... "I love you."

One... Genevieve's words filled Margo with the most painful happiness she had ever endured — painful, because she knew it would break, just like the water glass metaphor; tears of hurt and joy danced down her cheeks, as she kissed Genevieve as if Genevieve were the air and Margo were stuck on the bottom of the sea.

"I love you too"
she whispered,
when Genevieve
once again had
fallen asleep
on her shoulder.

91

3
Waking Up

When you wake up
from a dream, you
often do not care —

But what if you love
the dream so much
the reality can never
to the dream compare;

What do you do
when the dream is your life
and reality becomes
your life's nightmare?

Moments

It happened fast,
  and yet so very slow;

Margo was floating
  on the outside of her body
  watching her own lips smile
  while feeling her heart cry.

*At least everything is fine
  for a few more moments.*

She couldn't be more wrong.

Prey

Her chest is breaking
 literally breaking
 her ribs are cracking
 c r u m b l i n g
 like old wood in winter
 — *where is she?*

Genevieve is talking but
 Margo can't hear her;
 across the crowded gate
 on the other side of the
 thick wall of travelers
 a face appear.

Margo's blood is turning
 into icy snow, as the eyes
 that makes her organs
 twist and turn like worms
 inside her body, recognize her
 — *she is once again a prey.*

Him

"Where's mum?"
    is all she can say.

"She told me to come
    and get you, babe."

Him.

What the Fuck am I doing

"What's going on?" *Genevieve.*
"What are you doing here?" *Him.*
"Well, for your information..."
  Margo had to stop her.

"Alright, stop, stop!"
  What am I doing, what am I doing.
  "Genevieve, come with me,
  uhm, babe, I'll be right back."
  What the fuck am I doing.

The look on Genevieve's face
  when she went from confusion
  to slowly understanding; *pain.*

"No..."
"Genevieve..."
  Genevieve shook her head.

"No."

I Hate You

"Genevieve, please..."
"Are you serious, Margo?"
"I didn't know he would be here,
  I asked my mum to come get us,
  she must have..."
"I thought you left him."
"I did... well, no... it's complicated!"
"No, Margo, it's not, just explain..."
"He's coming this way,
  here's some money for the cab..."
"I don't need your fucking money,
  I need an explanation!"
"Please, not now, Genevieve..."

Margo pushed Genevieve away
 she pushed her happiness away.
"...I am so sorry."
 Please don't say you hate me.
"I hate you."
 I hate me too.

Throwing Hearts

His embrace made her
  want to throw up with
  all of her being.

"Looks like someone
  owes me a threesome"
  he grins while taking
  a hard grip around
  Margo's waist.

Why isn't he yelling,
why is he smiling?

Margo turned her head
  and saw Genevieve
  throwing the money
  for the cab on the
  ground, together with
  both of their hearts;
  stomped on.

Burning

A car window
  —*smash it, jump out, run!*
a boy she never loved
  —*tell him, leave him, flee!*
a hand with fingers gripping
the inside of one of her
inner thighs; *burning.*

Lemon Juice

Margo's phone started buzzing
  like a scared bumblebee trapped
in her pocket — *he turn his head.*

"So, you had fun on your little trip?"
  Lemon juice is dripping from his voice,
  his mouth still twisted in that crocodile
  smile — "Did you fuck her?"

"What... I..."
  It felt like his fingers were about to
  push through her skin — she could
  already feel the bruises blooming
  on her thigh — "No, no we didn't."
  He moved his hand to her face
  hooked her jaw in his hand —

"You're lying, babe."

Debt

Margo's phone stopped buzzing
the bumblebee is dead.

The hour home felt longer than
    the ten days with Genevieve
    — did that even happen?
    Everything is unreal.

He parked in front of the gate
    to her house and her heart
    breaks again (how many times
    can a heart break in one day?)

"So, what did we agree?"
"I owe you a threesome."
"Good girl."

Blood

He kisses her
  h a r d.

If he put his tongue
  in her mouth he
  would be able to
  taste her blood
   — but he didn't.

She kept biting
  the inside of her cheek
  until it was over.

Babe

She can't remember
  what she said or
  what she did but
  somehow Margo
  managed to make
  him go away.

"...I just think it'll be best if
  I try to handle my parents
  by myself, you understand,
  don't you... Babe?"

Can he hear her voice shaking,
  can he smell the vomit under
  her tongue when it forms the
  word "Babe"?

They said goodbye,
  she wished it was farewell.

The Storm

She walked up the stairs
  what will they say?
  she opened the door
  she can still run away!

Her mother embraced her
  her father — straight-faced;
  the calm before the storm
  — before being disgraced.

Schhh

Her father was yelling
  loud and long:

"Do you have *any* idea
  what lies I had to tell,
    to protect your reputation!"

"You *cheated* on that
  fine young man..."

Her mother: "Darling,
  maybe let Margo explain..."
  he *"schhh"*-t her —

"...and with a girl!"

Dog-lead

Margo zoned out —
  not on purpose, *of course*
  she did respect her father,
  her whole life had been
  circling around making
  him proud; *that's why*
  she could not yell back.

She wanted to, every cell
  in her body vibrated as
  a drill — *but she remained*
  quiet.

It wasn't fair, she knew that,
  she wanted to run out the door,
  call Genevieve — *but her father's*
  influence clenched her neck
  like a dog-lead.

Paper Cuts

Every letter and every word
  that he spit out of his mouth
  marked her mind and heart
  with deep paper cuts —

She left the room with a hundred
  hurting splinters of painful words
  stuck in her soul.

Lost

Margo was
  utterly
  completely
  fully
  entirely
  l o s t.

She crawled
  in under her
  white duvet
  and stained
  the sheets
  with grey
  rivers.

Black Stripes

Knock-knock.

It came from the window
  but Margo couldn't move.

Knock-knock-knock.

She sat up, slowly
  getting out of bed;
  stand up — walk.

Margo pulled aside the curtains
  and the memory from when they
  first met drowned her.

The girls face
  covered in black stripes
  from crying; only this time
  she wasn't smiling
  — *Genevieve.*

Wait

Margo opened the window
  and suddenly Genevieve
  was standing in front of her.

"Did you really climb
  all the way up to my window?"
  Really? That's all you say?

Genevieve didn't answer,
  she looked around the room
  her eyes landing on *his* sweater
  laying at the foot of the bed.

Margo was quiet now,
  couldn't speak, couldn't move
  — just wait.

Wait, and wait, and wait, and...
  Genevieve spoke.

What Genevieve Said

Genevieve is not the kind of person who loses control, she is not one to start yelling and throwing things — she knows how to handle her own temper. That is why, when she spoke, stinging shivers ran up across Margo's spine, because even though Genevieve remained calm, her voice, normally so strong and steady, was shaking:

"Yes, Margo, I climbed all the way up to your window, since something told me I am not enough welcomed here to use the front door — no, do not try to interrupt me, you broke my heart and I deserve to talk until I'm finished. Thank you.

I don't know if this was your plan all along, I have been walking around the streets these past couple of hours trying to understand. After you left me at the gate, I felt like throwing up. Literally, I felt sick to my stomach. Then, somehow, even after with my own eyes seeing you walk away with *him*, I figured that, no, there must have been a misunderstanding, you know? This can't happen. So I called you, to tell you I am sorry for saying I hate you. Well, I tried, you didn't answer. And when you didn't pick up, reality hit me again, and I didn't want to apologise anymore, because I'm not the one who should be sorry. I just want an explanation. I tried to brush it off, I called my dad and he picked me up, and I was *so angry,* Margo, I said that I never wanted to see your face again. But my dad thought I should try to reach out to you, one last time, so here I am. I refused at first. I decided to take a long hot shower, those always make me feel better, but this time I was just as empty stepping out of it as stepping in. So I took a walk. And I thought about the Chanel shoes you bought me. I thought about how easy you could just throw away money, and now I'm wondering if that is why you could throw away me so easily too. You can't see the value in things — or in people. Am I right? You just saw me as a get-away-ticket, a vacation from the huge lie that you refer to as your life. *I said don't interrupt me.* Eventually, I realized I wouldn't be able to let this go unless you make me understand why, so please, tell me. Tell me why this" Genevieve waved her hand between them "isn't worth fighting for."

Margo cried. They both cried. Though, unlike Genevieve, Margo could not speak while crying, and it all came out as sobs. Margo knew she was ugly when she cried, so she turned her head away, she couldn't face the girl she loved knowing the girl in fact hated her *and* saw the ugliest side of her at the same time. Genevieve on another hand was beautiful even now. Margo didn't deserve her.

"I'm a coward," Margo said after taking control over her voice. Genevieve just stared at her, so Margo continued — "No, I never planned this. I don't know what my intentions were, actually. I guess I was desperate, desperate to feel something... *more.*"

"And did you?"
"What?"
"Did you feel something more?"
"Compared to what I feel about you, Genevieve, I don't think I'll be able to feel anything at all in my life ever again."

Scared

"Do you love me?"

"Genevieve, we have barely known each other for two months, we haven't even *been* with each other for two weeks."

"Well, I love you, Margo. And I'm not afraid to admit that."

"But you're not afraid of anything, nothing scares you."

"Margo... *are you blind?*" the calm in Genevieve's voice started to burst, and her sunshine eyes turned into rainy clouds. "I am scared *right now!*"

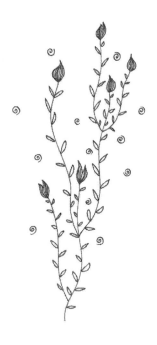

Bullshit

"Okay, Margo, then tell me you don't."
"Genevieve..."
"Tell me you don't love me, and I'll leave
  you alone."
"Genevieve, you know I can't do that."
"Margo, *please,* just say it."
"I'm sorry, really, I'm so..." *fuck, oh no,
  here comes the sobbing.* "s... so... so... sorry."
"Margo stop! Stop being sorry all the time,
  and do something! Stop saying that you can't
  because that is the biggest bullshit to ever
  escape your mouth!" *how can she speak
  in full sentences while crying?* "Stop worrying
  about what everyone else thinks about you,
  stop breaking yourself just to fit into other's
  expectations!"

*Genevieve is crying so much,
  there's so much tears.* Margo's chest crumbled;

I caused that.

Deep Breath

Deep breath. Deep breath.
 Take your voice back —

"I'm s... sorry fo... for all
 th...this. I mea... meant what
 I... I said..." *deep breath,*
 in — out. "I am a coward."
 You don't deserve her,
 look at her! You have to
 make her go away, you're
 only hurting her. "And lets
 be honest, you will get over
 me, this, us... You'll be over
 it all very soon, Genevieve."

As the last words hit the air,
 one could see how all energy
 left Genevieve's body, how her
 whole being relaxed in pure
 hopelessness. After staring into
 the wall for a while, she met
 Margo's eyes;

"What do you mean?"

Sad Chuckles

"I mean that... When we first met you cried because you had gotten your heart broken. But even that same night you took my number, and you were joking and... I guess what I am trying to say is, you'll get over it, soon. I've seen it."

Laughter. Genevieve was laughing. She was laughing so hard she had to sit down on the bed. But it wasn't real laughter, this was a desperate, panicking chuckling sound that soon turned into heavy sobs, and all Margo could do was watch. Watch and listen to how Genevieve went from laughing to crying to laughing to crying — *I broke her, I fucking broke her.* Genevieve was crying so much she almost, *almost* turned ugly. But she didn't. Even now, all wet and destroyed and with eyes wide open as if she were insane, *Margo still looked at her and saw beauty.* After a while Genevieve calmed down, and still sobbing, with a chuckle she said:

"You don't know shit about love, do you?"

When You Find Love

"Margo, when you find love you don't throw it away, not just like that, not like this. Okay, yes, I have had other girlfriends and *yes* I was completely heartbroken when we first met and *yes* I got over my last ex very quickly but... What you don't seem to understand is that every love is different, every time you fall in love you fall in love in a new way, every time you fall in love you fall in love for the first time and everytime you fall out of love or get dumped your heart will know a new kind of heartbreak — and this is the most painful heartbreak I have ever endured. My other relationships had one thing in common; the heartbreaks hurt because of disappointment. They hurt because of broken promises and shattered dreams but *this,* this hurt because of *everything.* Margo I..." Genevieve chuckled again while shaking her head. "I feel like I am genuinely going *insane.* My chest is physically hurting and I am so fucking lost and I don't understand and I am so very *very very* confused. This is not how you treat love, Margo, not when it's like this, not ever. Don't you feel it? Margo, it hurts, *it hurts so much.*"

I know, Margo's heart whispered. *I know, I know, I know, I am burning too.*

Hell

Hell is standing in front of someone you love while they are
in pain, knowing you are the reason why.

Razor Sharp

Margo wanted to
  take Genevieve's arms
  and put them around
  her shoulders and
  escape in the embrace
  — *but her father's*
  razor sharp words
  were still tied around
  her neck.

Breaking Up

"So, this is it then?"
no, no, no, no, no!
"I guess... yes. Yes it is."
it hurts, it hurts, it hurts
— Margo won't feel her nails
digging homes in her palm
until later when the hot
shower water makes the
small cracks sting.

"Well I..." *Genevieve's eyes*
are so empty. "I hope you'll
find what makes you happy."

I already have, and I am
pushing her away.

Goodbye

Margo cannot speak a word
   while Genevieve with shaking
   movements climbs out the window
   and jumps down on the ground.

By the open window Margo will
   stay, looking after Genevieve
   — seeing her happiness grow
   smaller and smaller and smaller
   and hours after Genevieve is gone
   Margo's blue lips will leave a silver
   whisper in the cold wind;

"I love you."

Old Newspaper

She fell asleep under
  the chilly dark blue sky.

The stars said goodbye
  and the sunrise said hello
  when Margo finally closed
  the window — *her heart.*

A fever flame had begun to
  swallow the insides of her head
  as if her brain was a wrinkly ball
  of old newspaper.

Monster

That next day
  he came by.

Margo had never been
  so thankful for being sick
  — *he didn't kiss her.*

He gave her chocolate
  and asked how she felt,
  and a bad conscious
  was infecting Margo's
  mind; *I cheated on him.*

Somewhere in the back of
  her head the memories
  of him were screaming;
  his jealousy, his hands,
  waking up in the middle of night
  with him i n s i d e —

But he was so nice now, so kind
  so soft, his voice drowned the
  images in her head and the only
  monster left was Margo herself.

Headache

Her eyes were slowly following the
  white flower pattern on the curtains.

The last words shared with *him*
  echoed in her head;
"Get well soon, babe, love you!"
"Love you too..."

Margo wasn't sure if it was the fever
  giving her a headache or if it in fact
  was the *love you* given to the wrong person.

Numbers and To-do-lists

Everytime she closed her eyes
  Genevieve's face was tattooed
  on the inside of Margo's eyelids.

With black spots dancing
  in front of her, Margo got up,
  walked towards her desk and
  pulled out a box — *a journal.*

It wasn't a pretty journal,
  it was old, and used and honestly,
  Margo didn't even remember where
  she had gotten it from. She only
  used it when she had to write down
  numbers or to-do-lists.

Back in bed Margo opened the journal,
  and soon its old sad pages were filled
  with something much more meaningful
  than numbers and to-do-lists.

28th August

I was never afraid of monsters under the bed as a child. Maybe because, as it turned out, I am a monster myself. A monster with a heart, apparently, or ~~who~~ why else would it pain me so much? I am so lost. And my head hurts. And I miss her. And you're just a journal so you don't know anything at all and I guess that's the point because I am planning on pouring myself into you now and you won't judge me. You ~~sho~~ should though. I have done something horrible and the worst part is, I don't regret half of it.

I don't regret it.

I do regret hurting her but I will never regret falling in love with her — Does that mean I actually don't regret hurting her either? But I do, I do regret it. I regret breaking her but I will never regret her.

Do I make any sense? I feel like I'm just rambling. I should get som sleep.

THE SAME DAY. (EVENING)

Honestly, I don't know what my point
with this is. I guess I just can not bare
keeping all this inside of my head. I've
been sleeping all day but I still can't keep my
eyes open — But I can't close them either.
Everytime I close my eyes she is there, I see
her when I'm awake and I see her in my
dreams; at least with my eyes open I can
try focusing on something else. Like... how
the empty ceiling reminds me of how
empty my body is, how the scissors on my
desk remind me of the cracks in my ~~heart~~
heart that ~~are~~ cutting my soul into pieces,
how the (sunshine) resting on my floor shows
glittery particles of dust dancing like we
danced in Paris the night of our first kiss,
how the window beside me is now filled with
dead insects entangled in messy ripped off
heartstrings... Who am I kidding?

I can't escape her, awake or asleep, eyes closed
or open — she will always be there. I will
find her in everything.

Is this my punishment?

29th August

I love my father. I do. I mean. He's my parent, how can I not love him? Of course I do. Even though his words have created a drowning whirlpool inside my chest and I can feel myself disappear in that hole deeper and deeper after every judgemental sentence — He won't shut up about it. I'm still sick, but I managed to eat dinner with him and my mother this evening. All he could talk about was my mistake. But he is wrong. I can feel it as a vibrating buzz under my skin, I know this isn't right, what he says isn't right; still I nod and apologise time after time. And I hate myself for it but somehow, when my father speaks, everything he says sounds true, and my head agrees with everything he says while my heart is screaming in protest. It's a confusing situation.

I love him but ~~oh my gosh I hate him~~.

30th August

Genevieve. I can't stop thinking about you.
And don't ask me why I am writing this as a
letter to you, I don't know, you will never read
it so it's kind of pointless, I know that. I guess
I just miss talking to you. Your name is ~~constantly~~
constantly whispering its letters inside me.
Inside all of me. It's such a beautiful name.

G - e - n - e - v - i - e - v - e

Such a magical sound. Your name is my
favorite word. It makes me think about cherry
lips and honey eyes and soft velvet skin
and sunshine laughter. Everything with you
is sunshine coated. Or at least it was.
Until I destroyed it. You said you were
going mad, well I am too. I am saying your
name with closed lips, pronouncing it with my
tongue without letting out any sound.
I miss you. I want you to be here.
I am pretending my pillow is your body and I
hug it all the time but you never hug me
back. Because you aren't here.

Just a pillow.

31st August

I took a bath today. First the water burned me, in my mind I saw myself stepping down in lava. I stayed so long the water became the same temperature as my blood, and then it became cold. And I stayed. Thinking about how easy it would be to bury myself under the blank surface. To never come back.

My thoughts started to scare me, so now I'm in my bed. Crying, again. It's been a lot of tears these past few days, I wonder when they'll run out.

I will stick to only showers for a while.

1st September

I tried to talk to my mother today. She is sleeping awfully alot. She always has been but I haven't thought about it before, it's just the way she is. But now I'm starting to think that she's not happy, maybe she isn't "just tired" all the time, maybe she actually... Is sad? It's so obvious when I look at her now. She always smiles when she's expected to smile, but whenever she doesn't think anyone is watching, her lips turn into drooping flowers. Anyway, I tried to ~~talk~~ talk to her. Ask her why she called him instead of picking me and Genevieve up from the airport herself, when I had asked her to. She never gave me a good answer, only short sentences about him being my boyfriend and that I shouldn't have a problem with it. When I tried to push out a better answer she said "You cheated on that fine young man, Margo. Be thankful he forgave you." ~~those were her words.~~ Those are my father's words. It was painful hearing them come out of her mouth, especially when her face turned into stone, growing harder and harder by every word — as if every word burned.

We were quiet for a while, just looking at each other. Then, my mother walked towards me and... hugged me. I don't know how to feel about this. She gave me a long, warm hug and I had to use all my strength so that I wouldn't start crying.

2nd September

I'm starting to feel better. I probably will be able to go to school tomorrow. I almost forgot about school. It feels so far away, still it is my everyday-day, with all my friends and routines and sitting in classrooms. Why is the feeling of going back there so foreign? It's only been one summer. As always. I really have to pull myself together.

I watched two movies today. First I saw "Gia" with Angelina Jolie. It was a wonderful, sad story. Then I watched a french film, "Blue is the warmest color" and it was, again, a wonderful, sad story.
Can't two girls have a happy ending?

Someday I am going to write a story about two girls with a happy ending.

3rd September

I went to school today. It was weird. My friends were drowning me with questions all day, most of them were upset while one of them asked me if I really love my boyfriend, and somehow I managed to brush it off and turn everything into almost nothing.

I turned my everything into nothing.

When the day was over, one of my friend stayed with me while I collected all my books. It was the friend asking me if I actually ~~love~~ him. She asked me if I'm okay. She seemed genuinely worried, instead of curious. I almost told her everything but I couldn't. So I smiled.

I smiled. Because that is what you do when you fall apart.

I said "I'm okay!"

And I know she knows I lied, and she knows that I want her to believe me, and I know she pretends to do just that, because she knows I want her to ~~be~~ believe me even though I know she doesn't.

4th September

This afternoon he came over. ~~He~~ wanted to have sex, and I panicked and said that I was on my period. I'm not.

5th September

I googled "Rape" today. This is the answer I found:

"Rape is a type of sexual assult usually involving sexual intercourse or other forms of sexual penetration carried out against a person without that person's consent. The act may be carried out by physical force, coercion, abuse of authority, or against a person who is incapable of giving valid consent, such as one who is ~~unless~~ unconscious, incapacitated, has an intellectual disability or is below the legal age of consent."

In the beginning, and throughout our whole relationship, I never gave consent but... I never said "no" either. Does that equal giving consent? Being quiet? And he had never had sex with me by carrying it out by "physical force" and he never threatened me, and I am capable of giving valid consent. But I guess being asleep is being unconscious. And, if I am being honest... he has a power over me, he's the one in control... so I guess... Abuse of authory?

Two. I have two pieces of evidence. "Unconscious" and "Abuse of authory" (?). But this is not evidence at all. I can get nowhere with this. It would be my

136

~~word~~ word against his, and the truth is...

I never said no. I am so confused. I'm scared. What do I do when I can't pretend to be on my period?

6th September

We went out shopping today. Me, him, a friend of mine and her boyfriend (who of course is a friend of his) and it was... Okay, I guess. I didn't enjoy it though. Normally I love shopping. I love pretty clothes and jewelry, but I felt nothing. I bought some things anyway, ~~boy~~ trying to be normal. But I couldn't stop comparing it all to shopping in Paris with Genevieve. Or just _being_ with Genevieve.
Everything is coated in this dull, gray fog without her. The only thing I was happy with buying was a new journal. It's much prettier than this one, it looks like a real diary. But I don't know what to fill it with quite yet, so I'm still writing in this one. Right, I kind of lost it when I got home today — I called Genevieve. I called her. But she didn't answer. I guess that's a good thing. I don't know why I did it, I didn't know ~~what~~ what to say I just... I had

to be close to her. I'm really trying to forget her, she probably already forgot about me and that's good.

I know ~~that~~ this is all my fault and that I have myself to blame but gosh it hurts. Will it ever stop?

7th September

I want to cut off my hair. But my hair is something I always get compliments for, it's one of my signature features. I guess that's a part of why I want to cut it off. To the shoulders, or more. My father would kill me though, I will never go through with it.

It's friday, and he's coming over tonight. He texted me this morning asking if my period is over. I told him not quite. I will have to sleep with him beside me, but... at least he won't be inside me.

I really don't want him inside me.

8th September

He ~~XXXX~~ left after lunch for practise, so I have time to be alone today. It's nice. I made it through a whole week of school with a broken heart and a burning bad ~~conscious~~ conscience, I guess that's something. Maybe I can do this.

I really want to know how Genevieve is doing. I know she's probably together with someone ~~else~~ who doesn't screw her over, but I still want to know. Or do I? If she's together with someone else it will hurt, if she's still in pain because of me it will hurt.

Why am I so fucking selfish? Of course I hope she found ~~someone~~ someone who deserves her. I do, I really do.

I'm trying to.

9th September

I can't lie about my period anymore,
and I'm going over to his place soon. Why
don't I just break up with him? It's so simple,
just... Why don't I just break up?

I looked through our social medias and the
pictures of us look so real, we look so happy,
everyone thinks we are so... perfect. We are perfect

I need to go now.

Breaking Steps

Every step leading to him
was another bone breaking
and by the time Margo was
standing by his front door
she was only a mere bag of
skin filled with grey dust.

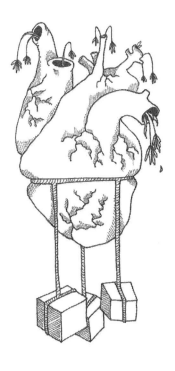

Rag Doll to Stone

i. They sit in his room on the bed watching Netflix on the big screen on the grey wall; *this is okay. This is nice.* His hands are on her thigh, moving their way up; *this is okay. This is nice.* Her heart is trying to escape out her throat, while ten fingers are invading her skin; *this is okay. This is nice.*

ii. Kissing. They are kissing each other. Or is it just him kissing her? She is moving her lips but it doesn't feel like she is kissing him back, it feels like she is giving meat to a hungry wolf so that it won't attack and devour her; *this is okay. This is nice.*

iii. A shirt, *her shirt,* being unbuttoned with a devilish force making the back of her tongue taste like vomit — "Stop... stop!" Confused he pauses for a second, before smiling and putting his whole weight on top of her. "Come on, babe, I'll make it good for you..." *this is not okay. This is not nice.* "...I know you have missed me too, relax..." *not okay, not okay, not okay.* "...you owe me this. This and so much more." *This is not nice.*

iv. Normally she would've just layed still, waiting; she endured it so many times already. But it was different now. Now she knew how things like these should feel like, and it shouldn't feel like *this.* It shouldn't be like this. Instead of letting her body turn into a rag doll as the countless of times before, she turned into stone.

vi. Why isn't he listening? She is pushing him off, but he only crawls back mumbling: "I've missed you so much, babe, I just love you so much, please stop fighting back, you know you want this, you love this, you love me..." his hands are too close, *they are too close.*

vii. With a hard push she makes him roll off of her, and she escapes the bed, hurrying to the door — but his body is pushing her against the wall, she hears how the rest of the buttons are landing on the floor, and somehow the small sounds are deafening, just like the sound of her stockings tearing apart with a heavy *ritchhhh!*

viii. She doesn't remember how she escaped that room. She doesn't remember how she slipped through his grip. She doesn't remember getting out of the house. She doesn't remember anything else but her bare feet on the asphalt, running and running and running and...

ix. ...*running for her life.*

4
Love

If hearts can break
and glass shards feel
then hearts can make
each other heal;

If love can lose
— shattering within
then love can chose
to fight, to win;

We tie together heartstrings
wishing for happy endings.

Buzzer

Margo rings the buzzer
  and a man's voice answers;
  "Hello?"

Heart pounding in her throat;
  "Sir, do you know Genevieve?"

Quiet. And then —

"I'm her dad, who am I talking to?"
"Margo."
"...I don't think my daughter wants
  to meet you Margo."
"Can you please let me in, sir."
"You hurt her, Margo..." *I know,*
  I know, I know. "...why should I let
  in the one who broke my daughter's
  heart?"

Do not start sobbing.
  She started sobbing.

"I need to meet her."

The seconds felt like forevers, bad forevers;
  the door opened and Margo run up the stairwell.

Oh

"Margo, *oh my God!*"
"I know, I know you don't want me here and I completely understand, but Genevieve just please listen..."
"What happened?"
"What?"
"Margo is that *blood?* Dad, is she *bleeding?*"

Genevieve's dad grabbed Margo's shoulders, softly but still hard, and turned her around so that he could look at her. His face, that had been filled with anger until now, was now covered with a layer of fear and worry; Margo looked down at herself and she finally understood why Genevieve had reacted as she did — Margo was barefoot, her blouse torn showing her bra and all over and around her breasts there was red scratches and growing bruises as if someone had painted her chest with lilac finger paint.

Only one sound escaped Margo's lips; "Oh..."

Yellow

They sat Margo down by the kitchen table
　and Genevieve's dad went away to fill up the tub.

Genevieve asked questions Margo couldn't hear
　and they ended up sitting quiet on each side of
　the table, with a small bouquet of yellow flowers
　between them; *yellow and sweet like our love*

...used to be.

New Made Tea

The water was hot like newmade tea but Margo didn't mind.
She could feel the nightmare dust from *his* fingers stuck on
her body slowly dissolve with the tiny bubbles dancing on her
skin — the shadow of his touch will forever haunt her, but in
daylight she will eventually be able to not feel the stinging
shivers from his *"Love."*

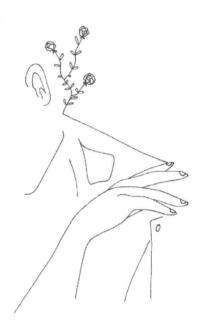

Guitar

Margo sits on Genevieve's bed wrapped in a huge bath towel (it's ridiculously huge; like an actual blanket) looking around the room. It's a beautiful mess. Like Genevieve's hair. Fairy lights hanging from wall to wall making the ceiling look like a starry sky. Margo looked out the window and remembered how late it was. The time must have been around ten pm when she ran away from him. Genevieve's dad was in the kitchen, giving them space but at the same time being ready to help — *like call the police, give her a ride to the hospital, anything* — but that wouldn't happen. Margo didn't want to call anyone. She just wanted to stay here, in Genevieve's star night room, forever.

In the corner between the drawer and the window a guitar stood against the wall, it was a really dark wood color with yellow and orange sunflowers painted here and there.

"Do you play?" Margo asks.

"And sing. You would've known that if you hadn't..." Genevieve shook her head. "Sorry."

If I hadn't left you.

Promise Me Something

"Margo, did he..."
"I don't want to talk about that."
"But this is *abuse* we have to..."

A loud, weird, high pitched sound
  escaped Margo's throat and she
  felt how she almost tripped over
  the edge of falling down in tears
  — *Genevieve turned silent.*

I left him, I left him, I left him,
  why do I need to talk about him?
  Why do I have to do anything?

"Okay, I just want you to promise
  me something, can you do that?"
  Genevieve said and Margo nodded.
  "Please, don't go back to him. I'm not
  asking for you to come back to me but..."
  Don't you want me back? Of course not.
  Silly me. Silly thought. Silly Margo.
  "...please, don't go back to that guy."

"Don't worry." Is all Margo can say.

The Tale of Margo and Genevieve

Genevieve looked through her wardrobe and took out a pair of grey sweatpants and a big yellow t-shirt with long sleeves and bumblebee prints and gave them to Margo; "I'll walk you home."

They are both quiet in the beginning of the walk. It's like a really strong rubber band is pulling them together but they both fight it, trying to walk side by side without touching, but sometimes their fingertips will get too close and both of the two girls are electrocuted by the fire raging in the air between them — *to have the one you love within reach but without touching them is a torture that deserves screams, but the night stayed silent.*

Margo asks more about Genevieve's music interest. And so Genevieve starts talking about how she as a three year old found her uncle's okelele and how music has been a part of her life since that very day. Sometimes she sings at the café where she works, and she is thinking of applying to a music college. Then Genevieve asks what Margo has been up too, and without a second thought Margo tells her about her writing.

"Really? What are you writing about?"
"Just diary entries for now, but I am thinking of writing a book."
"Do you know what the book will be about? Do you have a title?"
"Yes, I do..." and so Margo reveals the title of her unwritten book;

"The Tale of Margo and Genevieve."

A Question

"Will it have a happy ending?"
"I don't know yet. I hope so."

Make Me Shut Up

"Margo, what are you doing?"

"I guess... Genevieve I am so sorry."

"Margo *what are you doing?*"

"Can't we just keep walking?"

"What? *No.* Why did you come to me?"

"What do you mean?"

"Why didn't you run home?"

"Because... I missed you. I miss you."

"Do you have any idea of how much
it pains me to hear that knowing you
will slip away again? That I am walking
you home just to *lose you again.*"

"Genevieve, I am an idiot, okay? I am
a complete *fucking fool* and I am *sorry*
and *I miss you* and *I need you* because
every breath without you is like
wrapping my heart in a blanket of
stinging nettles!"

"You broke my heart, Margo, *you broke it*
and now you're back and I am confused
and I don't like being confused!"

"Genevieve I love you..."

"No. No, no. Shut up, Margo. *Shut up!*"

"Then make me shut up, Genevieve."

Never Worthy

Burning desperation and anger were at war with longing feelings balancing on shaking heartstrings; *hesitance —*

"Do it!" Margo screamed, tears starting to blur her vision. *"I love you, I miss you, I am a horrible person and I know that I will never be worthy of your love but..."* Genevieve didn't let her finish the sentence.

Found

Genevieve's lips met Margo's
and if their first kiss was a dancing ocean
this kiss was the eruption of a raging volcano —

Imagine all the things you have ever lost; this kiss contained the same overwhelming feelings as if you suddenly would find all those lost things again, all at once.

Their hearts conflate into one and the same, and there were no line drawn between their emotions which meant everything melted together into lava flowing in sparkling bloodstreams. If they could, they would merge into one single person, that is how desperately they clung on to each other, with every atom in their bodies (body?) shouting *do not let go!*

It was like coming home for the first time in forever, not knowing if they could stay, or if one heart once again would have to go away.

Tears

Genevieve is crying
  and when Margo kisses
  her tears away and asks
  what's wrong the answer
  she gets is;

"How do I know you won't
  break me even more?

How do I know you won't
  be too ashamed to be with me?"

How do I know you won't
  leave me again?"

And Margo takes her hand
  and whispers "I'll show you."

What Happened?
— *a summary*

He stood by the gate outside Margo's house. Margo had left her phone on his bed and he was there to return it, trying to laugh it all off and give her a kiss — and without thinking any further, seeing his face leaning down towards her, Margo hit her head against him as hard as possible, resulting in breaking his nose with her forehead.

"If you touch her again, I'll scream and wake up the whole neighborhood, leave, now." Genevieve said, stepping in between him and Margo. "Your bloody nose won't save you, her body is all bruised with your fingerprints, the only reason I'm not calling the police is because Margo asked me not to. *Fucking. Go. Away.*" And he actually left.

Margo sat on the ground shaking. *The night isn't over yet.* Genevieve wrapped her arms around Margo, holding her under the twinkling night sky. *The stars are rooting for them.* "I'm so proud of you," Genevieve said.

"Are you sure? Margo, I believe you, I promise, you don't have to..." but Margo shushed her and opened the door to her parents house.

"This is Genevieve. She's my girlfriend and I love her." A (painful) long story short; this house is no longer Margo's home. Once again, her mother did try to calm things down, and just like before, like always, her father made her keep quiet. Margo and Genevieve leaved with two bags and a suitcase.

Guilt

"I am so, *so sorry...*"
"Genevieve, please don't be."
"Margo, he *cut you off.* This is
  so wrong. How are you not
  more upset?"

Margo stopped walking,
  put the bags on the ground
  and placed one hand on
  each side of Genevieve's
  face — the love of her life
  was crying from guilt.

"Genevieve, please listen... hey,
  look at me, I am upset, of course,
  but I am also happy, I am so
  incredibly happy."

Happy

"How on *earth* can you be happy after all of this?"
"Because this horrible night gave me you back."

Duty

Margo moved in with Genevieve and her dad
  — she was forgiven.

They both said it was okay, that she could stay as long as she needed, but Margo couldn't help but to feel annoying; even though no one ever acted as she was.

She didn't know what to do with school, so she never went back. Genevieve tried to convince her otherwise but the risk of running into *him* was something Margo couldn't take. She couldn't. She never did anything about him, which made her feel shitty. She felt like she was a bad person, like it was her duty to *do something,* but she simply could not take the fight. Not now. Maybe not ever.

You are Brave

Later, Margo would understand that you are not a shitty person if you don't choose to take a fight. You already fought, and if you manage to leave, that is more than enough. You are not a shitty person for not wanting to run back to what hurt you, even if it's in the name of revenge and justice. Whatever you choose, you are brave.

The Café

Margo is now working in the café, together with Genevieve and three other people — Margo is still trying her best to remember their names. She is embarrassingly bad at remembering new names. But that's okay. She'll get there.

She got the job through Genevieve, obviously. Genevieve finally applied to a music colledge (and they will accept her, but no one knows that yet). Margo is clumsy at her job, but everyone is nice and understanding, and so she is learning more and more by every day.

A bell is ringing when the door opens, and a woman walks into the café. Margo's heart stops, and before the woman sees her, Margo sneaks into the kitchen with her heart in her throat. Her manager, a very kind man that reminds Margo of a big fuzzy bear, asks if she is okay. And Margo tells him.

"You should go out there and talk to her."
"Why?"
"Because you will regret it otherwise. I'll let you work a little longer tomorrow if you want to, don't worry, now go out there. Trust me."

And so Margo goes out of the kitchen, enters the café and walks up to the woman. The woman's eyes are filled with tears, and she gives Margo a long, long hug. After a few confused seconds, Margo hugs her mother back.

Weeds

They sit down in a corner next to a window,
  they order one coffee and a hot chocolate
  and the girl serving them (god, Margo wish
  she was better at names) told them that it's
  on the house.

Margo asks what her mother was doing there,
  and her mother's response made Margo choke
  on her drink, making her lungs burn.

"I am leaving him."

It all ended with them both crying, Margo's
  mother telling Margo how proud she was of Margo,
  and Margo telling her mother that she is proud of her too.
  They're proud of each other.

They cry, and laugh, and exchange "sorry"-s.

There will be toxic people in your life,
  and even though weeds can be beautiful sometimes,
  sooner or later, you'll have to rip them out of your garden
  if you want anything else to bloom.

Not Yet

Margo's shifts often end when Genevieve's begin,
  so it soon became a habit for Margo to stay there
  until Genevieve got off work —

Margo was writing on *The Tale of Margo and Genevieve*
  every spare minute she got. Mostly she sat in the
  café after work, with a hot chocolate by her side
  and Genevieve used to come by while working and
  give Margo a kiss or two, and sometimes
  a new cup of hot chocolate.

"Can I read it?" Genevieve asked every day
  and every day Margo had to laugh and say,

"not *yet*."

No Sugarcoat

Margo sat on Genevieve's bed, writing. Genevieve's dad was out with a friend, and Genevieve had been away all day checking out the music college she got into (told you).

The Tale of Margo and Genevieve made Margo cry and laugh, and sometimes she thought of leaving some bits and pieces out, but figured that, no. This is their tale, and no matter how sweet and blissful their love is now, their story is not to be sugar coated.

So Margo wrote down everything. She had been writing for months now, and she could feel how the end got closer and closer and... now it's here.

Honey

The front door opens and —

"HONEYYY, I'M HOOOME!"

Genevieve comes rushing into the room and suddenly Margo's head is deep pushed down in a pillow and Genevieve is kissing her, *she tastes like bubblegum.* Then she asks Margo if she can read the tale;

"Wait, I have a girlfriend on my face," Margo says and untangles herself out of Genevieve's hug. "Also, do you have to yell *every* time you get back home?"

"Oh, shut up, you love it."
"Okay, yes, I do."
"So, can I read it?"
"No, but you can help me."
"Your princess in shining armor is here."

To End

"Okay, so I have written it all down now, like it's pretty
  much   done, but I have no idea on how to end it. How do I
  end it?"
"Why don't you just end it as you want it to end?"
"Yes, but... Shouldn't it be realistic?"
"What does realistic mean?"
"Shouldn't I write something about, I don't know, that no
  matter what happens, no matter if this lasts or not, I'm still...
  Thankful?"
"Margo, do you hear yourself?"

Margo buried her face in the pillow, giggling.
"It sounds so *cheesy* and *cliché* yes, yes *I know* but what do I do?

Fuck Realism

Genevieve was quiet for a while, then she took Margo's notebook and pen, turned over to a blank page, and said:

"You know what? Fuck realism."

And so she scribbled down the last lines of their tale.

I Love You

Margo read the messy ending of their tale
  and her heart melted into round, soft crystals;
  she kissed Genevieve, mumbling "It's perfect"
  and Genevieve kissed her back, and they laughed
  and they were in love and everything was
  warm and fuzzy.

"I love you."
"I love you too."

And they lived
happily ever after ♡

Thank you

I want to say thank you to everyone who helped me on this journey, everyone who gave me feedback and ideas on how to improve this little tale.

A special thank you goes to my wonderful friend Anna Zakhary, who helped me with my english grammar, since I still have a lot to learn, and who loved Margo and Genevieve from the very start. Thank you so much, Anna, this book wouldn't be the same without your help. *(You can find Anna on the instagram-account: @thebestpoets)*

And last but not least, thank you. Thank you to everyone who is holding this book in your hand. I hope you enjoyed reading it just as much as I enjoyed writing it.

Also by Sallie Lundh:

Dissection of an Eggshell Girl

Instagram: *@poetic.ligation*

Made in the USA
Middletown, DE
01 June 2018